I ARISE

I ARISE

Against All Odds, I Arise

TEDRIA DENISE

Cover design by Studio 5 Agency

Book design and production by Keen Vision Publishing, LLC

Editing by Keen Vision Publishing, LLC

ISBN-13: 978-0692658116

(Keen Vision Publishing, LLC)

To my family and the destiny helpers that
God strategically placed in my life. To
anyone who has experienced hardships.
You are unique. You are special.

Live your best life,

Tedria

About the Author

Tedria Denise was born and raised in Harvey, Il. Searching for love in the wrong places led her to have her first of 5 children at the age of 15. Becoming a teen mother quickly changed her perspective on life. She worked hard not to become a stereotypical teenage mother. She graduated with honors and was accepted in the Who's Who Among High School students for her achievements. She eventually earned her BS in Business Management from Indiana Wesleyan University. Tedria served in the area of special education within the school systems of South Bend, Indiana, and Indianapolis, Indiana for over 17 years. She has served in various church leadership roles. Her employment history is complimentary of her multitudes of talent. She loves to sew, write, draw, teach, and watch movies. She also loves to sing and dance even though her family teases her about her lack of talent in those areas. She is an entrepreneur, Certified 5D Identity Coach, Certified Human Behavior Consultant and is currently pursuing a Masters in Psychology with an Applied Behavior Analysis concentration. She currently resides in Indiana with her five children and grandchildren.

Contents

Introduction

How long will you hide behind the fake smiles, the nice clothes, the fabricated social media posts, and forced public displays of affection?   When we experience painful encounters, our first reaction is to suppress. We would rather forget it than to live with it. We paint the pretty picture, using shades of orange, yellow, white, and green, steering clear of the painful reds, the confusing grays, and the dark blacks. When people ask about our lives, we only tell the beautiful story, share only happy moments, and never speak of the situations that crushed our spirits. We want everyone else to have the comfort of thinking our lives have been nothing short of perfection while we toss and turn nightly because of the demons we have protected. It isn't until we finally realize that there is freedom in their exposure, there is liberation in our truths, and that there is healing in revealing, that we begin to open our mouths and speak. It is at that moment that everything that has held us bound can be used for the strengthening of our spirits, and the genuine improvement of our lives.

Step into my closet. I'm not talking about the nice and neat closet where I allow my guests to hang up their coats. I'm talking about the closet in my backroom. The closet full of things that I can no longer use, the dark places of my soul. The things I am no longer ashamed to admit I own. The things that have shaped me into who I have become. The things that broke me down, but built me up. The things my family are not

even aware of.   The things that no longer have the

power to hurt me because they have been exposed.

Walk with me as I share my innermost secrets. Walk

with me as I am set free. Walk with me as I arise.

1

WHAT GOES ON IN THE HOUSE,

STAYS IN THE HOUSE

In the beginning, my life was the typical American dream. My parents were married and had two kids, a boy and a girl. We lived in a beautiful white, two-story home. Our home was nestled in a beautiful neighborhood of hardworking families. I loved our house. It had four bedrooms, a basement, an attic, and a nice-sized backyard. The living room had pretty ivory carpet. We had a white sofa and loveseat with green flowers. They were perfectly upholstered with a plastic covering for protection. We had a long box stereo that had a turntable and an eight-track tape set.

On the weekends, daddy played Al Green and some of the other old school guys. I loved hearing that music play throughout the house. My brother and I shared a roomy bedroom. Our bedroom had two twin-sized beds, one on each side of the room against the wall facing the door, with a small TV in the middle. Our bedroom had plenty of space for us to play with our toys, but our favorite place to play was in our back yard. Our backyard was the envy of many of our neighborhood friends. We had many things to do in our backyard. Daddy had even built us a zip-line. It was so much fun to play in our yard.

My parents were different in size and personality. My dad was a proud countryman. He was a big, burly man who didn't mind speaking his mind. My mother, on the other hand, was often very timid. She was a tall, slim woman who often suppressed her feelings and her thoughts. For a young black couple in those days, my parents had done well. Daddy was from the south. He built a wonderful lifestyle for our family with only a 6th-grade education. From the outside looking in, we had a perfect life. For a while, my brother and I didn't have a care in the world.

One day, I heard my parents arguing. First, they went back and forth about something I couldn't quite make out. Then, I heard my mother whimpering and begging my dad to stop. I peeked into the living room and saw my mother lying on the floor trying to break away from my dad who was on top of her. My heart froze. It was daylight outside; they knew we were awake. Why on earth would they do this to us, I thought. I quickly ran back to the hallway to catch my brother before he walked in on them. Unfortunately, I found him standing in the hallway outside of our bedroom with a blank look on his face.

"James, stop. The kids…please stop," my mother cried from our living room. I quickly guided my brother into the bedroom. I turned on the TV hoping to drown out the sound of our parents' voices. We sat on the floor, and I rocked him gently in my arms.

"It will be okay. It will be okay." I whispered to him.

The image of my dad's huge body on top of my mother's small frame haunted me. Even when I tried to sleep at night, the image would play back and forth in my mind like a one scene nightmare. Sometimes, I would be wide awake, and that same image would flash across in my mind. I would blink and shake my head in hopes to erase that dreadful image from my mind. It never happened.

I have many memories similar to this one. After seeing my parents on the floor that very first time, everything else began to make sense. I remember the day I became even more aware of what was happening between my parents. Even though it was decades ago, one day in particular still resonates in my mind. It was a beautiful day. I could hear the birds in our yard chirping. The bright rays of the sun burst through our large living room window, creating a lovely warm look inside our home. Terrence and I played as our parents talked in the kitchen. Momma was preparing dinner, and we couldn't wait to sit at the table and eat her delicious cooking. Suddenly, I heard my father yell out to us, "Go outside and play. Stay in the yard!"

Terrance and I didn't think twice. We put on our shoes quickly and ran out of the side door to our back yard. We rode our bikes and played on the zip line. We were having a blast. I needed to go to the bathroom, so I headed back to the house. Before I went in, I reminded my little brother to stay in the yard.

On my way up the stairs, I saw my mother. She seemed skittish as she ducked off into the kitchen. I saw my dad walk off into their bedroom. At first, I didn't pay attention to them, but when I headed back outside I noticed that my mother was in the kitchen with a towel covering her nose. I no longer desired to go outside and play, but I knew that I needed to protect my brother, so I ran back outside to play until it was time for dinner. That embedded vision of the day I saw her on the floor under my dad flashed through my mind. I began to link that current moment to all of the other times when we were sent out of the house to play. I realized that each time he sent us outside to play it was to hide what was going on inside the house.

It became clear to me that even though my dad loved us, he was hurting my mother.   As a child, I couldn't understand why she put up with it. As an adult, I can look back and realize that my mother endured so much so we could continue living the "good life", but as a child, I began to dislike my dad. Daddy was a true provider, and he had never hurt my brother or me. He was like a big loving teddy bear. As a child, I knew that Daddy worked hard to take care of us and get us the things we needed and even the things we wanted. I knew that we were blessed. We never wanted for anything, but I would have gladly given up everything to stop dad from hurting my mother.

2

I KEPT YOUR DIRTY SECRET

Oh, how I loved our family reunions. We usually had a family reunion once every summer. It was always a blast. We got to meet Daddy's family. He had tons of brothers and sisters from the south that would come up to visit us. Daddy was born in Little Rock Arkansas, but he also had family in St. Louis, Missouri. When he was a teenager, he moved to Illinois. Some of his siblings also moved to Illinois and created similar lifestyles like my dad, while some of my father's siblings believed in living life on the wild side. I loved my funny and crazy uncles. They made us laugh so hard. Life was so much fun whenever they came around.

There is one family reunion that I will never forget. I remember waking up and seeing that sunlight beaming through the living room window. It warmed me up like always. I was truly excited about having a good time with my family. My mom picked out a maroon outfit for me to wear. I could not wait to put it on. I jumped out of bed and realized that my mother and my aunts had been up all morning cooking. Our house smelled delicious! The aroma of greens, cornbread, and boiling potatoes made my stomach growl. I couldn't wait for our family cookout to begin. My mother and one of my aunts were in the kitchen

cooking while another aunt was sitting at the table talking and keeping them both company. Dad and his brothers were outside barbecuing. My brother and I decided to go outside and play. That day, we met more of our first cousins, several of dad's brothers and their wives. There weren't many kids. Our cousins were teenagers. They were young men. So the younger kids laughed, partied, and ate, as the grown ups drank and had "grown folks" talk. We were having so much fun; the day flew by. Before we knew it, it was late, and everyone had to say their goodbyes for the night.

My brother and I went into the house to prepare for bed. We took our baths and put on our pajamas. I had on a pink and white, long princess nightgown. It was one of my favorites. We were excited to find out that one of our first cousins would be spending the night with us. We rarely had company so we were excited to have our big cousin over. Daddy said he could stay in our room. My brother and I slept in the same bed. I sleep on one end of the bed, and he slept on the other end. Our cousin slept in the other bed.

I went to bed happy and exhausted. It did not take me long to fall asleep. Suddenly, something startled me. I did not feel right. I felt like I was drifting in the air. At first, I thought I was dreaming. I was so tired; I could barely open my eyes. I realized that I had been removed out of my bed, and someone was holding me in the air. I felt something hard rubbing on my inner

18

thighs and touching my private area. In fear, I shut my eyes tight. I remember trying to peer through one of my eyes to see what was going on. When I realized that it was my cousin, I was confused. I didn't understand what he was doing, but something told me that I shouldn't let him know that I could see him. He held me and continued to rub his privates on me fast and hard until he exploded all over me. The look on his face and the way his body shook like an earthquake scared me. I squeezed my eyes shut even tighter. He couldn't know that I knew what was going on. He gently slipped my panties back on me, pulled my princess nightgown back down and put me in my bed.

The next morning, I thought what had happened was a dream until I saw the evidence all over my thighs. Then, I knew what had happened the night before was real.

"Good Morning, Nookie, my cousin said to me, as if nothing happened. Nookie, that's what dad's family called me. As a child, I couldn't understand what he had done, but I knew it was wrong. I knew no one was supposed to mess with my private parts. I was confused because he acted as if everything was okay. How could he smile at me, I thought. How could he act as if nothing happened? How could he laugh and joke with me as if he didn't violate me the night before? It confused me. My first thought was to tell

Daddy. I knew that if I did, Daddy would be upset, and our family reunion would be over. I didn't want to ruin the fun for everyone else. My mom already had enough on her mind. So I made the decision to keep his dirty little secret. From that day on, I lived my life as if I had slept through the whole night; as if I had not felt my body move or felt him touching me, or that I peeked open one eye to see what he was doing to me. I went on with my life as if it did not happen. I allowed my cousin to think that I slept through the night. I told no one. But the truth of the matter is, I remember what happened to me as an innocent little girl. The image of my cousin was added to that of my mother and father.

On the surface, I never allowed the incident to stop me from living life or enjoying our family reunions. I pretended like nothing ever happened. While I didn't know it at the time, keeping my cousin's dirty secret would cost me more than I would ever know.

3

THE GREAT ESCAPE

My brother and I came home from school to find that our long, canary yellow Buick convertible had been packed with our belongings.

"Get in the car kids," my mother said.

"Where are we going, mommy?" we questioned back

"For a ride, just get in the car so we can go," she responded.

I didn't know it at the time, but she was trying to hurry up before my dad came home from work. We were obedient and got in the car. I looked at my mother, and there was something different about her and her demeanor on that day. She wasn't quiet and timid like we often saw her around my dad. She was happy and anxious. I could tell she was trying to make this experience an adventure for us. She kept the top down on the car as we rode down the street, past our school, past the car dealerships, BOZO Hotdogs, Dairy Queen, and the South Suburban College. She pointed out different places as we enjoyed the breeze and the beauty of the day. After we had driven for a while, we pulled into a parking lot of a hotel. Mom went into the office, talked to the people there, and came back out to the car. We drove away from the office and parked in front of one of the hotel doors. She unloaded some of the things she had in the car and began taking them inside. She had saved her money from work to pay for a one month stay at the hotel. My mother had escaped. I was so proud of her. She finally got away from Daddy. As a young girl, I remember thinking about how brave my mother was. I wondered if she was nervous. I wondered if she worried about him looking for us. I was afraid of what he would do to her if he found us. I knew my dad loved us, but he had a problem. He hid it well, but my mother had gotten tired of being his punching bag. She made a stand. Even though we didn't have our nice house and big backyard, I was at peace. I didn't have to worry about my brother walking in on them fighting. I could sleep at night without worrying about what was going on in

the next room.   We were free.

4

THE ADVENTURE

Our adventure continued, and Mom tried hard to keep our day-to-day routine. She still went to work at the hospital part-time, and we still went to school. She drove us to school everyday before work. Some days we had to stay in the hotel by ourselves for a couple of hours. We had specific rules to follow. Mom gave us exact details on what to do in case of an emergency. I was the oldest, so I was responsible for my brother and following all the directions she left. We were way too young to be staying in a place like that by ourselves, but my mom did not have any other help. I wondered what happened to my father. He loved us

27

so much, so I know he had gone looking for us. We never saw him or heard from him for a while.

Mom had only saved enough for one month's stay in the hotel. Soon, we could no longer afford to stay there. One day, she folded all our clothes and packed all our things back into that canary yellow Buick, and we left the hotel.

"Mommy, where are we going to go now?" I asked.

She said the same thing she said to us before. "Just get in the car and ride."

Finally, we made it to one of her friend's house. My mom's friend let the three of us stay in one of her spare bedrooms. The lady had a child, but we never got to play because we were always gone. My mom kept our routine of work and school. We were gone most of the day.

Out of the blue, we had to leave. My brother and I were asleep. It was so late. I overheard the lady saying to my mother "I need you to leave now." You see, the night before, my mother had a male visitor in the room we all shared. I remember hearing them whisper. I suppose mom thought we were sleep. The lady was not happy about it at all. I faintly heard her fussing with my mom about the fact that she had a daughter that stayed in the other room and that it was not okay for her to be bringing a random man into her home.

The thing that bothered me was that I was sure I'd heard that man's voice before…before that evening …

before we moved out of dad's home.   I didn't know it at the time, but his voice would become a familiar sound I would grow to hate.

My mother did not argue, plead, or beg the lady to stay. She simply gathered all our things with a straight face and left. Once again, we were on the road in that canary yellow Buick. It was dark. I couldn't see where we were going. All I could see was the bright colors of the street lights, business signs, and the light from other cars on the road. We finally arrived at the home of another friend. This place was different.   It only had one bedroom, so we slept on a pallet in the living room.   It didn't have a lot of space, so we kept our things in the car.

Our routine continued. At this place, we became friends with the lady and her two children. I had fun playing with her daughter's hair braiding it in different styles.

One day, mom decided to do something special for us with some extra money she had earned.

"How about we do something fun tonight!" She said. We were very excited. All of us, including her friend and her kids, piled into that canary yellow Buick. We went to a drive-in movie theater. It was like an enormous football field. There were cars everywhere parked in sections and rows. Each section had a huge screen facing the opposite direction. Each screen played different sets of movies. We could hear the movie through a big sound box the attendants gave us to hang in our car.

It was too chilly to let the top down on our convertible, so mom let all the back windows down. We had a blast taking turns hanging out the window, sitting on the ledge of the door. We watched movies until our eyes could not take any more. When we woke up, we were on the pallet in the living room of the little place we shared. Even though it wasn't much, we were happy. We were so grateful for my mother's friend.

5

THE BOARDING HOUSE

Our happiness was short-lived. One day, the landlord gave mom's friend a notice. He knew she had someone else staying in the place, and that was not allowed. It was time to pack again. This time, we moved into a boarding house. It was a two-story home with a bathroom and several rooms upstairs. It belonged to an older white woman, and she rented my mother one of the upstairs rooms. The room was shaped like a big square. It had hardwood floors, one bed, a dresser and a TV. It wasn't much, but it was somewhere to lay our heads. My mother tried to make the room as comfortable as she could. I liked that it

33

was our own little space. We didn't share it with anyone. It was like staying in a section of a dollhouse. I liked the quiet room.   It had two large windows with pretty curtains that welcomed the sunlight each morning. It reminded me so much of Daddy's house.

Like any siblings, my brother and I liked to goof off sometimes. Well one particular day, my brother was doing something that irritated my mother. She asked him to stop several times before she finally raised her arm with the belt to spank him. He fell to the floor, scooted, and his head fell back. All of a sudden, we saw blood. Mom helped my brother up, and I looked at the back of his head and screamed. She swung him around. The back of his head was split wide open deeply. Mom grabbed a towel and placed it on the back of his head to slow the bleeding. I was scared. His head was bleeding heavily. I didn't understand why his head had split open until I looked at the floor and noticed a huge nail sticking out from the wood. Mom gathered our things, then told me to hold the towel to my brother's head. My heart was beating hard as I held the towel on his head and held him in my arms. I comforted him and told him everything would be okay. We got in the car and rushed to the hospital. When we got to the emergency room, my brother and I sat down as my mother went to sign him in. There were a lot of people in the emergency room. We waited for hours, and I began to worry about my brother. I asked my mother why we had to wait so long. She explained that there were a lot of people who needed help. My mother spoke very calmly, but I saw the worry in her eyes. As a child, I couldn't understand why they would allow us to sit in the emergency room for so long. My brother needed help. After what felt like eight hours, a nurse finally called us into the back room. She took his vitals and got more information from my mother about what happened. By the time the doctor came in, my brother's wound was hard and dry. The doctor had to squirt the wound with saline to clean it and stitch it up. I squirmed at the thought of the pain my brother endured. If only they had called him back sooner, I thought. Since I was just a child, I shut my mouth and held my

brother's hand as the doctors patched him up.After

they had finished, we headed home. It had gotten

pretty late. As soon as we arrived at the boarding

house, Mom put us to bed, and we slept through the

night.

The next day, the old white woman scolded my

mother and said we had to go. My mother sighed.

Again, she didn't argue or plead her case. She packed

our things in the car. This time, we didn't ask where

we were going. This time, she didn't have to say get

in the car. My brother and I had gotten used to the

routine. This adventure was not fun anymore. I was

tired of moving from place to place. I just wanted a

place to lay my head and call home.

6

NEW BEGINNINGS

I remember the day things started to get better for my family. It was a beautiful fall day, and the weather was so nice. It wasn't too cool, and it wasn't hot. The sun shined brightly. The leaves on the trees had turned into the most beautiful shades of orange, burgundy, and yellow. For some reason, this day seemed extra special. My mom dropped us off at school all cheerful and happy. She smiled at us, wished us a good day and gave us her normal rules. We went to Bryant Elementary School. It was a two-story school. The office was located on the first floor. We loved that school. It was right across the street from a high school. Sometimes, we could hear the high school marching band practice. We loved to hear them play.

After school, we walked with our friends and followed mom's directions on where to meet her. When we met her, she was still as excited as when she dropped us off at school.

"I have a surprise for you all," she exclaimed.

"What is it?" we asked.

"Oh, you have to wait and see!" She smiled.

As we drove further and further away from the school, our curiosity got the best of us, and we couldn't be still. We kept looking out the windows, switching sides with each other.

Finally, mom pulled in front of this apartment building. It was a set of two apartment buildings with a big parking lot in the middle. She parked the car. We all got out, and she guided us to the very first apartment on the lower floor of the two-story apartment building. She used a key and opened the door. To our surprise, all of our things were in the apartment. My brother and I ran in and began to check the place out. With excitement, mom gave us a tour of the place. It was small, but it had a living room, kitchen, bathroom, and one bedroom. She took us in the bedroom, and we leaped with joy at the sight of our beds, dressers, clothes, and toys. I was so excited. Our superhero had saved the day again. We stood there hugging each

41

other. We finally had a place we could call home. It was ours. We did not have to share. We didn't have to worry about anyone kicking us out in the middle of the night. I looked around and noticed that my mother didn't show us where she would sleep.

"Mommy, where are you going to sleep?" I asked.

"Right here!" She smiled.

She took us to the sleeper sofa in the living room and showed us how it converted into a bed. She had put her clothing in the hall closet where the coats would normally go. She explained that as long as her babies had a room, she would be okay.

"Mommy, but how? How did you do this?" I wanted to know.

"Daddy helped me with the apartment and your things." She explained.

What? Daddy? I didn't say it out loud, but I sure thought it. Mom had run out of options and went to the person she had escaped. Even though we were no longer in his house, our daddy still loved us. Moments like these made me love him so much. I forgot all about how much he had hurt mom and desired to see my dad again.

Later that day, my dad stopped by. When we saw him, we jumped on him and gave him big hugs. We were so happy to see him. He spoke to my mother and told her to let him know if she needed anything else.

My dad had moved out of the house we shared as a family and into another home not too far from the school we attended. Some days, we walked to his home after school and mom picked us up from there. Some days we had to catch the city bus. Yes, the city bus. We were very young, but mom said we could handle it. She showed me where to walk, which bus to catch, and where to get off. She took us to the bus stop and followed the bus to show us where it would go and where to get off.

I was very nervous on the days we had to ride the bus, but I knew I had to be a big sister. I did exactly what Mom said. I guided my brother and watched over him. He trusted me and always followed my directions. He never questioned me. My brother was skinny, quiet, and timid. Some even called him a cry baby. I loved him so much. He was my heart. When I found out that he was being bullied, it made me very upset. Terrance told me that an older boy had been picking on him. Terrence showed me the boy, and I planned how I would let him know that my little brother was not the one to pick on. One snowy day after school, I saw the boy walking by himself. There was no one else around that I could see, so I tackled him. He looked up in shock. I straddled over him and pinned him down. When I looked down, I could tell that the boy was very afraid. I looked him right in his eyes and warned him never to bother my little brother again. When I felt that he had gotten the message, I let him up. The next day I saw him with his sister. She was bigger than me, and I just knew she was about to get revenge for her younger brother. As I walked past her, my heart raced. To my surprise, she simply looked at me and said hello. Weirdly enough, we all became friends and walked with each other after school.

Everything seemed to be going really well until the day our school secretary called me into the office. Some adults began to ask me a bunch of questions about how I got to school, where I lived, who I lived with and so on. When I got home, my mom asked me what happened at school. I told her that I was called me into the office, and I gave her a rundown of everything they asked me. After I was done, she explained to me that we couldn't go to our school anymore. We would have to transfer to a school close to where we lived. I was so disappointed. I was so upset with myself for not realizing what the adults at my school were doing. I was angry that they had taken advantage of me. There was nothing I could have done about it. We had to move to a new school and make new friends. It seemed like we would never be able to settle in anywhere. Some days, I wished that we were back home with Daddy, living perfectly, imperfect lives.

7

MEN WERE HER KRYPTONITE

Supermom did it again. It had been one whole year since we escaped from Daddy. Mom told us that our lease was coming to an end. I didn't think twice about it because I didn't know what that meant. One day, our mom met us as we were heading home from school. She led us to another apartment in our complex. We were very confused. I had had a long day at school, and I just wanted to go home, go to my room, and relax. We walked hesitantly behind her. She finally stopped at a door, opened the door, and walked in. We stood outside the door, and she beckoned us to come in. We walked in, and the apartment had been furnished with all our things. In one day, she had moved all our things and set it up in a whole new apartment. This apartment was bigger than our old one, and it had two bedrooms, one for her and us. Her bedroom was really nice. She had a big bed, a long dresser with a mirror and a little table on the side of the bed with a lamp. She explained to us that our other lease had run out, so she applied for a bigger apartment in the same apartment complex. I never knew how she did it, but I was glad she did. We were happy to have a place with two bedrooms. Mom needed her space.

Something was different about her. Mom was changing, and I didn't like it. One night at our other apartment, I woke up in the middle of the night to go to the bathroom. I got up and noticed that our bedroom door had been closed. I almost opened the door until I heard a familiar man's voice. I stood there for a few seconds and realized it was the same man that I heard at our mom's friend house. It was the voice that had gotten us kicked out in the middle of the night. I tapped on our bedroom door and called my mom. She told me that it was okay to come out, and thanked me for warning her first. When I walked out the room, I glanced over to my mom's sleeper sofa and noticed a man tucked under the covers close to her. I was glad that she finally had her own room.

Though a lot of things changed about her, she was still a mother to us. She gave us strict rules to follow. As we got older, her rules became even more strict. We were not allowed to go outside when she was at work. We had to do all our school work and complete all our chores before playing. Whenever we did go outside, we had to be back in before the street lights came on. We followed her rules and did what she said. Mom's timidness had gone away. She was different. Her desire for companionship overtook her and men became her kryptonite. They drained our superhero. She brought different guys to our apartment, and she still made Daddy think that he had a chance with her. I began to grow angry and frustrated with her. Several times I would come in the house and hear noises coming from her bedroom. At first, I didn't know what it was, but then it became very obvious because her moans and groans were really loud. They were so loud that I could hear them outside her bedroom even with the door closed. I was too embarrassed to even bring my friends inside. Anger would often boil inside of me. My heart would race, and I would bang on the door at her and her company.

I'd scream, "Why! Nasty! Why! Get out, why are you here? Leave!" She would totally ignore me like I wasn't there. One day I got up the nerve to confront her. I asked her if she would refrain from doing her business in the middle of the day. I explained to her that it was embarrassing to have my friends over as she

carried on with her company in the other room. After

I had pleaded my case, she didn't explain anything to

me. We didn't have a talk about the birds and the

bees. She didn't tell me to stay out of grown folks'

business. She simply said, okay. I remember feeling

like I wanted to scream. What had happened to my

superhero?

8

OUT OF CONTROL

Things soon got out of control. My superhero lost her balance. One night I was awakened by loud noises. My mother was yelling my father's name and begging him to stop. For a moment, I thought I was dreaming. I ran out into the hallway, and a man ran past me out of the back door. It was that same man again. My dad was beating and yelling at the front door. Someway, daddy made his way in. She ran out and around the apartment with her long nightgown on. I was glad that it was late, so no one could see what was going on. At first, I decided to go back to bed and pretend that I was sleep, but I didn't. I stayed up. Dad had been giving

mom money to help out with the bills with the

assumption they would work on things. When daddy

found out that the guy was coming over, he was

furious. If only he knew that the man who ran out

wasn't the only man. Mom was also seeing a guy

named Tye. Tye was obsessed with mom. He would

flip out on her and yell at her whenever she threatened

to end the relationship. One time he even chased the

car and grabbed at the door while she was driving.

Things got progressively worse with every chance she

gave him. One day, he threw hot water on her face

and burned the left side of it by her temple and eye. It

was bad and left an ugly burn mark, but she eventually

faded it with special creams. I was furious. My mother was a beautiful woman; her skin was flawless. The only makeup she ever wore was lipstick because that was all she needed. I asked her why she allowed Tye to hurt her, and she told me not to worry about it. Even though I was young, I had seen enough to know that something was wrong with this man. How could she tell me not to worry about it? I made up in my mind that if my mother wouldn't speak up for herself, then I would.

Several days after the attack, he showed up to our apartment to patch things up with my mother. I answered the door. In height, I was at his chest, maybe a little bit taller, but I didn't care. I looked at him and told him to leave.

"What!" He shouted at me.

"Go! You hurt my mom. You burnt her face. I should burn yours with the iron for what you did!" I shouted back.

"Do what you need to do!" He replied.

That made me even more mad. I looked at my mother for support, but she sat there with a blank look on her face. I stormed back to my room with my friends. He barged in, directed his attention to my mother, and asked her for another chance. When she told him no, he slapped her hard. It was so hard, my friends and I heard it in the other room. I ran into the living room and yelled at him. My friends grabbed me and told

me that we could get their parents to help. We all ran

through the alley that led to the other street where they

lived and told their mom what was happening. She

called the police. We all came back to my house, and

I told Tye that the police were on their way. He found

his way to the back door and scurried out of there. I

never saw him at our place again after that. My mother

was shaken up, and I saw that innocent, vulnerable

look on her face. She looked at me and thanked me

for being so brave. I looked at her. My heart was

broken. Where was my superhero? Where was my

brave mother who had escaped my father's abuse? I

realized that now I wasn't just my brother's protector. I was my mother's protector too.

You would think that my mother had learned her lesson, but she didn't. While she was dating crazy Tye, she also entertained married Tyi. How she ended up dating two different guys with the same name, I don't know. We began getting obscene phone calls from his wife. She eventually she figured out where we lived. One day we came home, and the side view mirror was hanging off the car. She had snatched it off with her bare hands. Before that happened, Tyi's wife had assaulted my mom at the grocery store. The situation became very uncomfortable, unsafe, and embarrassing for my brother and me. My closest friends knew about what was going on, and some thought it was pretty funny. They got together and devised a plan to do prank calls to my place pretending to be the wife. They would call at crazy times of the night, curse my mother out, and hang up. I was pretty clever at figuring things out. I dialed *69 to find the number. They weren't even smart enough to block their number, so I quickly found the number did not belong to Tyi's wife. I never confronted them about it, but I began to distance myself from them. I didn't understand how they could play such a cruel joke on my family. As time went on, I silently forgave them. The sad reality was that each of our families secretly battled with something. In the end, we were all we had. We understood that we had to stick together.

My mother finally wised up and got a private number. She also got a restraining order against Tyi and his wife. The unfortunate thing was that Tyi was a pretty nice guy trapped in a very abusive relationship.

As time went on, my brother and I began to spend more and more time outside of the house. We went to friends' houses, played outside, went to the pool, or hung out at the skating rink. We were hardly ever at home, and mom didn't worry about us. We made sure we were home before the street lights came on, but during the day, we did whatever we could to stay away from the drama my mother entertained.

9

WHERE IS THE LOVE?

We lived in our apartment for several years until mom got approved for housing assistance. We moved into a townhouse not far from the apartment. I remember being so excited about the move into the townhouse. It had three bedrooms and a basement. My brother and I had our own rooms! It was so sweet to have my own room, my own space, and my own closet. I loved sharing a room with my brother, but we were getting older. We needed our own space.

At the time, my mother was dating a guy named Donald. Donald was several years older than her. I didn't understand why my mother wanted to be with

Donald until I heard her talking to one of her friends

about him. My mother stayed with Donald because

he was caring and giving. She felt she could grow to

love him. To me, they had nothing in common.

Donald would rather lie in bed with her than go out

somewhere. My mom was the complete opposite. She

wanted to go out, have fun, and dance. Being who she

was, my mother eventually found someone she could

have that kind of fun with. Donald would stay with us

sometimes. Everything my mom told her friends about

Donald was true. He took really good care of my

mother. He gave her money for the bills, he was nice

to her and even gave her a car. Even though he was a

great provider, I didn't care for him.   He always seemed so weird and sneaky. Every morning, he would come into our room to wake us. It made me so uncomfortable to wake up to him shaking my back. One day, I felt his hand a little too close to my butt. This angered me. I finally told my mom that I wanted to wake myself up. I never told her why. She told Donald, and he no longer came into our rooms to wake us.

As a teenager, I had developed a nasty attitude. I was always defensive. I was prepared to defend myself if ever I felt like someone was trying to take advantage of me. My teenager attitude made things difficult between my mother and I. The more I developed into a young lady, the more I felt she couldn't stand me. Sometimes I felt my mother didn't want me around. We would get into heated arguments and scream at each other nonstop. Most of the time, she would just ignore me. I would get so frustrated that I would slam glass plates on the table. I would even grab a knife and begin to cut myself in front of her. Nothing I did mattered. It's like she knew I was only acting out for attention, and she refused to give me the attention I sought. I couldn't understand her. All I wanted her to do was grab me, hold me, and tell me that she loved me. I wanted her to comfort me and tell me everything would be okay. She never did.

I began spending days and nights away from home. Sometimes I would stay at our next door neighbor's house. Other times, I would stay at my friend Donna's house. Her mother didn't mind at all. Donna had a brother who was a year older than me. We all would hang out and watch tv, do homework, or just talk. Donna's brother was handsome. He was tall and slim. I called him "Dark Hershey Chocolate" because his skin was so dark, pretty, and smooth. He had dark eyes and deep sideburns. We caught each other's attention, and it became clear that we liked each other. Donna's mom noticed our attraction and quickly reminded us that we were like brothers and sisters.

Of course, neither of us paid attention to her. We began to spend more alone time together. At first, things were innocent. I would sit with him and watch tv, or lay my head in his lap as he rubbed my back. One day he kissed me. I felt something I hadn't felt before. Of course, I'd had other boyfriends before. In fact, I had my first boyfriend when I was eight. We talked to each other out of our bedroom windows when our parents were not at home. I had the biggest crush on him, but the relationship was innocent. This relationship with Donna's brother was far from innocent. With my mother doing her own thing, and my brother not really being old enough to have the same interests as I did, I accepted Donna's brother,

Darren, into my life. The more time we spent together,

the more things got heated. One night, he and I hung

out in his townhouse. There was no one else around.

He told me how much he loved me, and I felt in my

heart that he was telling the truth. I loved Darren. We

began to kiss, and he slowly removed my clothes.

That night, I lost my virginity to him. We began to have

sex all the time. We sneaked away from our parents.

Whenever I would begin to talk to him about the

things I dealt with with my mom, and everything else

in my life, he would seem uninterested. It became

evident to me that I was not Darren's only girlfriend. I

ignored it and made myself believe it wasn't true. I

continued to have sex with him. He was my escape.

He made me feel wanted and loved. He gave me the

attention I so desperately desired. Even though he

really wasn't interested in me, his sexual attention was

better than the complete lack of attention I received at

home.

10

ADULT ACTIONS BRING ABOUT

ADULT RESPONSIBILITIES

Months before Donald and I began having unprotected sex, I had started my period. My cycle was irregular. Sometimes I would go almost two months without a period. Without my mother's guidance, I never understood the dangers of having unprotected sex. I was so naïve and foolish. Darren was older than me, so I just trusted him. After missing my period for almost three months, I figured something had to be wrong. I went to Darren, and he completely flipped out. He started yelling about how he had pulled out and how there was no way I could have missed my period. I was so confused, and I didn't understand what he was talking about. Well, I guess he told his mom, and she told mine. One day, my mother informed me that she was taking me to the doctor to get a checkup and put me on birth control. Our visit to the doctor's office changed my life forever.

"Ma'am, your daughter is pregnant." The doctor informed my mom.

"How far along?" my mom asked.

"I am not sure because of the irregular cycles," he explained.

"She may be six to eight weeks."

My mother told Darren's parents, and both families got together to arrange for me to have an abortion. They felt that we were too young to have a baby. Our education came first. My mother took me to the abortion clinic on the scheduled day. I sat as they prepped me for the abortion. Just as the doctor was getting ready to do the procedure, he stopped and informed my mother that I was too far along to have the procedure. The baby would be born in a few months. My mom didn't frown. She had that same straight face she had when we were kids moving from place to place. We left the abortion clinic and went to a thrift store. She bought as much as she could for the baby. She explained to me that there was nothing else to do but prepare for the baby's arrival. I felt closer to my mom that day than I had felt in years.

As time went on, my pregnancy began to show. People slowly found out about my pregnancy. Older women in the stores would turn up their lips and make comments under their breath as if I couldn't hear them. Rumors began to spread around my school. It was difficult to walk down the halls with people staring and pointing at my huge belly. My home life was even worse. Without Darren's attention, I was without a companion. My mother was never home. She was always out doing her own thing with her male friends. One of her male friends even asked my mom for a threesome with me. When she told me what he had said, I looked at her with disbelief. I wasn't shocked by his request, but more so that my mother stayed with him. By this point, I had lost ALL respect for her. I loved her, but I did not respect her. In my gut, I wanted to hate her, but I never could bring myself to hate her. No matter what, she was still my mother.

I kept myself occupied by focusing on school. I was an A Honor Roll student. Even though I was pregnant, I went to every single class until it was just about time for me to have the baby. A few of my teachers respected my drive and made sure that when it was time for me to have the baby, I had all of my class assignments. When I could no longer walk the long halls or climb the flight of stairs to get to class, a couple of my friends would take my assignments to my teachers for me.

In the warm month of May, my baby boy was born. I was 15 years old. I was no longer just a young teenager. I was a teenage mom.   I had the responsibility of another life in my hands. I vowed I wouldn't be like my mother. I made it my mission to love him selflessly. My plan was to do well in school so that I could graduate, pursue a good career, and provide for my son. I pictured Darren and I raising our son, like one big happy family. A real happy family, unlike what I experienced. Unfortunately, things were harder than ever for me. I didn't have very much support, so I had to push myself. Every day, I would remind myself of my goals, my mother was no help at all. I would get up early to dress my son, and get him ready for daycare. Teen pregnancy was common, so our school had a program for teen mothers. My son's daycare was right across the street from the school. I was able to go and check on him at lunch, and then get back to my studies.

I had so much to learn about being a mother, in addition to being a teenager, student, sister, daughter, and a lady to a guy I was crazy in love with. I was on birth control, and we were still active. I called myself being careful and doing the right thing as far as taking the birth control, but apparently, I wasn't doing it right. I became pregnant again my senior year of high school and had a little girl. I wanted to beat myself up about it, but I didn't let that hold me back. I pressed even harder. My hard work in school paid off tremendously. Not only did I remain on the honor roll, but I also received the honor of citizenship and was listed in the Who's Who of High School Students.

Financially taking care of my children was a battle. My mother got government assistance and food stamps for all of us, me, my brother, and my children. I hated it. Even though she was getting the money, I still had to care for my kids and buy the things they needed. She would aggravate me so much. She would wait until they ran out of diapers to buy more, then would pay for a small box of diapers from the corner store when we could have gotten a bigger box for cheaper at the Aldi's. She would take the money and buy my kids raggedy hand-me-downs, but buy herself nice clothes. My mother was always dressed. She had a closet full of suits, dresses, pants, and shoes. It was clear to me that my mother was self-absorbed. I decided to take a stand for myself and my children.

My school also had a program where I could work and get credit. I signed up for it so I could get the things the kids needed without waiting for my mother. I needed my mother's permission, of course, she refused to sign. She said that it would affect her government assistance. So, I signed it for her. My mother was not in a state of mind to make adult decisions. So, I made it for her.

My first job was at a family grocery store. I found a friend from school that lived across the street from the store to watch the kids for me. She only had to watch my son, because my mother would always keep my daughter. Oddly enough, my mother wouldn't let my daughter go to daycare, nor would she allow me to take her out. It was very weird.

After getting that job, I felt liberated. I didn't have to depend on anyone to get the things I needed for my children. My children's grandfather was an awesome man. He was like a dad to me. He would help me whenever I needed something. Their grandmother was supportive as well. She taught me how to cook some of her specialty meals. At times, she treated me like I was her own daughter. Darren's sister, Donna, found stability and structure with her dad. I always looked up to Donna. She was so smart and always found happiness in spite of what was happening between her parents. Their family dynamics may not have been perfect, but they accepted my children and me. My children and I lived with Darren and his mother for awhile. Things were hectic, but I was grateful to have a place for my children and me to lay our heads. One day, my children's grandfather drove out to the apartment we were staying in and told me that he wasn't going to let me waste my life. I was months away from graduating. I wasn't going to quit, but I took a longer maternity leave than I did with my son so that I could work. Their grandfather was not having it. He had me to pack up all our things, and he took me to my mother's house. After my mother had turned us away, he took us to his place. We stayed with him until one of the apartments in the complex he owned became vacant. He told me that I could live there with the kids and pay him rent. God had really blessed us. I had my own apartment and that same year I graduated from high school. My mother began to see me in a whole different light. She was amazed at how determined I was. She began to respect me. I guess I reminded her of who she used to be. After graduating, we slowly began to restore our relationship. I remained consistent and worked hard to give my children a better life than what I had experienced.

AUTHOR'S NOTE

AGAINST ALL ODDS I ARISE

Our childhood experiences shape majority of our adult life.   Reflecting on my own childhood helped me to bring clarity to a lot of the experiences I've had in my adult life. As adults, we tend to think kids will be too little to remember or that they won't be affected by what they see or hear. We sometimes even believe that the things they experience as a child will not affect their futures. This is a lie. This memoir is proof of the many things I hid deep within me. Though I tried to forget it, they affected my very core. My childhood traumas influenced my adult decisions, and now MY children have hidden dark memories, even though I fought hard to prevent this.

After hearing the idea of my story, my writing coach (who is also my publisher), suggested that this book would be a book of healing for me. At first, I did not see it that way. I thought I had already healed and that everything in this memoir was in the past. But the more I began to write, the more I realized that I had not yet healed. I had never truly dealt with my childhood experiences.

After completing this book, I could see where instances in my life had repeated. Some of the things that my mother experienced, I went through in my own life. When we fail to properly deal with these rotations, they become generational curses. I want to

encourage you to take some time and review your life.

Look deeply into cycles and ongoing pain. I decided

to share this memoir with the world because I know

that there are many adults who experienced similar

issues growing up.   Often, we feel alone in our

struggles.   Many of us grew up in a time where we

were told to be quiet, and keep things a secret. We

were subconsciously taught to suppress our emotions.

In our culture the thought of counseling is asinine. As

a result, many of us are sick, hurt, and broken as adults

because of the trauma that took place as a child.

Personally, writing this book has created a greater

bond between my children and me. As I shared my

life story with them, they began to understand why our lives happened the way it did. I even took the time to acknowledge the things my experiences had done to them and apologize. I urge you to take this same step of healing with your family. For us as parents, grandparents, uncles, aunties, and so forth to not raise a nation of dysfunctional adults, we must acknowledge that it is time for deep down healing to take place within us. It is time for the shackles of our pasts to be broken. It is time for us to acknowledge the root of our innermost issues, deal, forgive, release, and allow healing to begin.

Declare It

As you begin a journey of healing, speaking these declarations over your life daily. I stand in agreement with you that healing is indeed taking place in your life, and the lives of the generations to come.

I declare and I decree that all pain and hurt from the past has been released.

I declare and I decree that a supernatural healing is taking place in my life.

I declare and I decree that my children and my children's children will no longer be unconsciously affected by the trauma of our past.

I declare and I decree the chains are broken and I am FREE. I am free from the bondage that held me back from becoming all that I was designed and created to become.

STAY CONNECTED

Thank you for purchasing I Arise, I Arise: Against All Odds I Arise.   For further information on booking Tedria for speaking engagements, new book releases, or updates on Author Tedria Denise, please visit the following connection outlets.

TedriaDenise.com

Ru.juststylin@gmail.com

Periscope: @juststylin4life

Facebook: facebook.com/juststylin4life

Twitter: @juststylin4life

Instagram: @juststylin4life

www.ingramcontent.com/pod-product-compliance
Lightning Source LLC
Chambersburg PA
CBHW062014040426
42447CB00010B/2019